AF228617

Vermont

BY CASEY ENGLUND

CONTENT CONSULTANT
Paul Searls, PhD
Professor of History
Northern Vermont University

An Imprint of Abdo Publishing
abdobooks.com

abdobooks.com

Published by Abdo Publishing, a division of ABDO, PO Box 398166, Minneapolis, Minnesota 55439.
Copyright © 2023 by Abdo Consulting Group, Inc. International copyrights reserved in all countries.
No part of this book may be reproduced in any form without written permission from the publisher.
Core Library™ is a trademark and logo of Abdo Publishing.

Printed in the United States of America, North Mankato, Minnesota.
052022
092022

Cover Photo: Shutterstock Images
Interior Photos: Jenna Brisson/Shutterstock Images, 4–5; Red Line Editorial, 9 (Vermont), 9
(USA); Toby Talbot/AP Images, 10–11; Ann Ronan Picture Library Heritage Images/Newscom, 13;
Shutterstock Images, 18 (flag), 18 (flower), 34–35, 40; Christopher Crosby Morris/Shutterstock
Images, 18 (horse); Mircea Costina/Shutterstock Images, 18 (bird); Nancy Kennedy/Shutterstock
Images, 18 (tree); John Couture/Shutterstock Images, 20–21, 45; Brian A. Wolf/Shutterstock Images,
26–27, 43; Christian Ouellet/Shutterstock Images, 29; James Kirkikis/Shutterstock Images, 31;
Townsend James/Shutterstock Images, 32; Wangkun Jia/Shutterstock Images, 38

Editor: Marie Pearson
Series Designer: Joshua Olson

Library of Congress Control Number: 2021951564

Publisher's Cataloging-in-Publication Data

Names: Englund, Casey, author.
Title: Vermont / by Casey Englund
Description: Minneapolis, Minnesota : Abdo Publishing, 2023 | Series: Core library of US states |
    Includes online resources and index.
Identifiers: ISBN 9781532197871 (lib. bdg.) | ISBN 9781098270636 (ebook)
Subjects: LCSH: U.S. states--Juvenile literature. | Northeastern States--Juvenile literature. | Vermont--
    History--Juvenile literature. | Physical geography--United States--Juvenile literature.
Classification: DDC 974.3--dc23

Population demographics broken down by race and ethnicity come from the 2019 census estimate.
Population totals come from the 2020 census.

CONTENTS

THE GREEN MOUNTAIN STATE

Snow crunches beneath the hiker's shoes. She reaches the top of Mount Mansfield and looks out. This is the highest mountain in Vermont. Wind whips against her jacket. The Green Mountains spread before her. Pine trees dot the landscape. It's no wonder Vermont is known as the Green Mountain State. The hiker continues down the trail. It is quiet. She's one of the only people on the mountain.

Vermont has many tree-covered mountains, which make the landscape green.

MUCH TO OFFER

Vermont is in the New England region of the United States. This region includes the six states in the northeastern part of the country. The region's name refers to English settlers who began building new homes there in the 1600s. New England played an important role during the Revolutionary War (1775–1783). The state is bordered by New Hampshire in the east, Massachusetts in the south, New York in the west, and Canada in the north. As a result, many Vermonters have close ties to Canada.

American Indians have lived in Vermont for thousands of years. French explorers arrived in the 1600s. The name *Vermont* comes from two French words meaning "green mountains." Mountains make up just part of the state's natural beauty. The state also borders Lake Champlain in the northwest. This is one of the largest lakes in the country. Many of Vermont's towns and cities are located near the state's beautiful natural scenery.

PERSPECTIVES
CANADIAN NEIGHBORS

Tom Powell lives in the Burlington area. The nearest big city is in a different country. So when Powell wants to experience city life, he hops on the highway and heads 97 miles (156 km) north to Montreal, Canada. He is just one of many Vermonters who enjoy close ties with Canada. Some extended families are spread across both sides of the border. Many northern Vermonters have Canadian friends. Businesses in the area also rely on customers from the other country. Getting across the border is typically quick and easy.

Vermont is a small state. Fewer than 644,000 people live there. Many people live in rural areas. Burlington is Vermont's biggest city. Nearly 45,000 people live there. It is one of many cities near Lake Champlain. The state's biggest college, the University of Vermont, is located in Burlington. The city is known for its beautiful buildings.

Montpelier is the state capital. It is located on the Winooski River in a valley between mountains. Rutland is another one of the state's bigger towns. Its location near lakes, ski resorts, and trails makes it a popular place for outdoor enthusiasts.

In part because Vermont has a small population, it attracts many tourists. They come to enjoy the state's open spaces and old-fashioned charm. Vermont remains a unique attraction for many people. Whether it's the welcoming small cities and towns or the scenic natural beauty and outdoor activities, the state has much to offer.

MAP OF
VERMONT

Vermont's geography is defined by its rivers and mountains. How do you think these features affected where European settlers started their cities? What evidence for this can you find on the map?

HISTORY OF VERMONT

People have lived in Vermont for thousands of years. The area's earliest known inhabitants are called Paleo-Indians. They arrived between 11,000 and 9,000 years ago, following the last Ice Age. The land the Paleo-Indians inhabited was unrecognizable from today's Vermont. Much of the state was still covered by the saltwater Champlain Sea. The people never stayed in one place long. They moved to where they could find food, such as mammoths, caribou, whales, or seals.

As the land changed over the following millennia, people remained in the area. The modern Abenaki are descendants of these peoples. The Abenaki's historical territory was the area east of what is now called Lake Champlain.

Life in the cold, northern climate could be harsh. The Abenaki came to value the plants they could grow for food there. They also ate animals such as moose and deer. The people often traveled throughout the area using birchbark canoes or snowshoes. In the 1600s as many as 10,000 Abenaki people might have lived in the area. Other peoples, such as the Mohicans and Mohawks, also lived there at this time.

EUROPEANS ARRIVE

By the 1600s Europeans were beginning to settle in North America. Samuel de Champlain was a French explorer. In 1609 he became the first European to see

Lake Champlain, which was named after him. However, it wasn't until 1666 that the French established the first European settlement there. Fort Sainte Anne was on Isle La Motte on Lake Champlain.

The first permanent European settlement was Fort Dummer. Massachusetts lieutenant governor William Dummer was one of a group of people who purchased the land in 1716. The settlement was built in 1724. It was near today's Brattleboro in southeastern Vermont. More settlers moved in after that, often from Connecticut and Massachusetts. By the time of the

Revolutionary War, approximately 20,000 Europeans
lived in Vermont.

The Europeans were coming to an area where the
Abenaki and other American Indians already lived. The
settlers and American Indians sometimes got along.
However, the settlers increasingly encroached on the
American Indians' lands. With greater numbers and
powerful weapons, the settlers forced the Abenaki out
of their villages. Some American Indians retreated north
to Canada. Many died from European diseases such
as smallpox and measles. Others eventually joined the
European settlements. However, their ways of life were
forever changed.

THE ROAD TO STATEHOOD

Vermont was not one of the original 13 British colonies.
Instead, it was considered a territory. Both New York
and New Hampshire claimed it. This conflict caused
tension. Many settlers had been granted land by
New Hampshire. When New York began issuing titles

to the same land,
the Green Mountain
Boys pushed back.
This militia formed
to protect people's
rights. It aggressively
resisted New York's
claims. That dispute
was put aside in 1775,
however. That year the
Green Mountain Boys
helped capture Fort
Ticonderoga in New
York from the British.
This was one of the first
American victories in
the Revolutionary War.

Vermont soldiers
went on to play an
important role in

PERSPECTIVES

ETHAN ALLEN

The government of New Hampshire granted land in Vermont to Ethan Allen. When New York began issuing competing land titles in Vermont, Allen took action. He helped form the Green Mountain Boys in 1770. The militia guarded properties from New Yorkers. It also attacked settlements that had been granted by New York. Allen described these actions as protecting "liberty, property, and life." He continued to resist New York's claims after the Revolutionary War. He at one point tried to have Vermont join Canada instead. Many historians do not think he actually wanted to join Canada. They think he was trying to get Congress to accept Vermont as a state separate from New York.

the war. And when the British accepted defeat in 1783, the 13 colonies became the first 13 states. Vermont, however, was not part of the new country, nor was it part of Britain. Rather than joining the United States as part of New York, Vermont declared itself an independent republic. This period lasted until 1791. Finally New York gave up its claim to the area. Vermont became the fourteenth state. The episode was seen as an early example of Vermont's tradition of independence.

Vermont grew rapidly in the years following statehood. Trains began connecting it to nearby states. This helped new industries thrive. In the early 1800s, mining began to flourish, attracting immigrants who were looking for jobs. By the 1900s Vermont began changing. For decades people had been leaving the state for opportunities elsewhere. The state needed to do something to keep growing. So it turned to tourism. State officials began promoting Vermont's rural charm. Developers built ski areas in the mountains. People began building cabins and hotels across the state. These changes helped tourism become a defining characteristic of Vermont's economy.

GOVERNMENT IN VERMONT

Today Vermont's government is divided into three branches. The Senate and House of Representatives make up the legislative branch. They create and change laws. A governor and lieutenant governor are elected to lead the executive branch. The governor signs bills into law. The judicial branch, or the court system, determines what the laws mean and applies them.

QUICK FACTS

There are many things that make Vermont unique. How do these facts help you understand Vermont?

Abbreviation: VT
Nickname: The Green Mountain State
Motto: Freedom and Unity
Date of statehood: March 4, 1791
Capital: Montpelier
Population: 643,077
Area: 9,616 square miles (24,905 sq km)

STATE SYMBOLS

State animal
Morgan horse

State flower
Red clover

State bird
Hermit thrush

State tree
Sugar maple

The United States does not recognize any American Indian tribes in Vermont. But the state of Vermont recognizes four Abenaki tribes. They are the Elnu Abenaki Tribe, the Nulhegan Band of the Coosuk Abenaki Nation, the Ko'asek (Co'wasuck) Traditional Band of the Sovereign Abenaki Nation, and the Abenaki Nation of Missisquoi. These recognized tribes can receive help from the state of Vermont to preserve their languages and cultures. They continue to help shape the state's history and culture today.

FURTHER EVIDENCE

Chapter Two covers the early history of Vermont. What is one of the main points of this chapter? What evidence is included to support this point? Read the article at the website below. Does the information on the website support the main point of the chapter? Does it present new evidence?

THE ABENAKIS & THE EUROPEANS

abdocorelibrary.com/vermont

GEOGRAPHY AND CLIMATE

Those visiting Vermont today will find lush mountains and beautiful rivers. That is very different from what the area looked like 500 million years ago. At that time the state was covered by a tropical ocean. Around 400 million years ago, Earth's shifting crust changed Vermont's landscape. This movement closed off the ocean and forced rocks to form into mountains.

Glaciers also played a major role in Vermont's geography. These huge pieces of ice and snow once covered the entire state. Approximately 14,000 years ago the glaciers melted, creating lakes and river valleys in the process.

Much of Vermont is part of the Lake Champlain Basin. Water in this area drains into Lake Champlain, the state's largest lake. It is 120 miles (193 km) long. Its widest point is 12 miles (19 km) across.

The Green Mountains in the state's center are part of the Appalachian Mountains. Pine and maple trees cover

ON LAND AND IN WATER

Vermont's plentiful lakes, rivers, and ponds make ideal homes for North American river otters. These playful creatures often live in burrows near the water. The burrows can have many tunnels. An adult male river otter typically weighs from 10 to 33 pounds (4.5–15 kg). Webbed feet help the river otters swim. Thick fur helps water slide off their bodies. River otters can sometimes be seen sliding down hills into the water. However, they're not always easy to spot once in the water. That's because a river otter can hold its breath for up to eight minutes.

the mountains and give them their name. Many rivers throughout the area shaped the valleys by eroding parts of the mountains.

Vermont has four seasons. It has spring, summer, fall, and winter. Warm but short summers give way to cold and snowy winters. However, different parts of the state experience some variation. The mountainous parts of the state tend to be the coldest. In the west, near Lake

PERSPECTIVES

FARMING IN VERMONT

Jon Cohen owns Deep Meadow Farm in eastern Vermont. He grows vegetables such as tomatoes, kale, beets, and onions. The growing season in Vermont is short. Cohen begins planting his seeds during the winter in a greenhouse. When the ground outside thaws, he moves the seedlings outside. The summer growing season is very busy. There aren't a lot of workers in the area to help. Because of that, Cohen and other local farmers usually bring in seasonal workers from countries such as Jamaica. Cohen said to Vermont Public Radio, "Our friends from Jamaica who work for us, they are critical components for ourselves."

Champlain, temperatures stay milder. The warmest temperatures are often found in the southeastern part of the state, which has a lower elevation and no major bodies of water nearby. Blizzards sometimes cover parts of the state in deep snow. Other kinds of extreme weather, such as tornadoes, are less common than in other parts of the country.

PLANTS AND ANIMALS

Various types of plants and animals thrive in Vermont. Many of the state's 2,800 plant species are flowering plants. Grasses and shrubs are common. Thick forests cover nearly 80 percent of the state. Beech and birch trees grow in these forests. The most common tree is the sugar maple. Nearly one in five Vermont trees is a sugar maple.

The forests provide homes for small animals such as squirrels, weasels, and foxes. Large animals such as black bears, deer, and moose thrive in Vermont's forests too.

Many bat species take advantage of Vermont's caves and mines. However, several are threatened by white-nose syndrome. While bats sleep through the winter, fungus grows on the bats' skin. The fungus irritates the bats, causing them to wake up. Animals that sleep through winter do so to preserve fat. Being awake causes the bats to use up their fat stores, which can lead to death.

EXPLORE ONLINE

Chapter Three discusses Vermont's plants and animals. Every source includes slightly different information. Visit the article at the website below to learn more about Vermont's wildlife habitat. What information presented here is similar to Chapter Three? What is something you learned from the website that was not in the book?

VERMONT'S WILDLIFE HABITAT

abdocorelibrary.com/vermont

RESOURCES AND ECONOMY

Vermont's industries have changed since the first European settlers arrived. Early settlers were mostly farmers. Today the state's economy is more diverse, with people working across many industries.

One industry that has stuck around is mining. Many early immigrants to Vermont were drawn to jobs in quarries or mines. People from Italy often worked in the granite quarries around Barre in central Vermont.

27

Welsh immigrants were common in the state's slate mines. Both types of mining were similar to what those people had done in their home countries.

Mining remains an important industry in Vermont. Stone quarries can be found throughout the state, extracting many minerals. The Barre area continues to produce granite. In other parts of the state, people mine for marble, slate, sand, and gravel. These products are then used in construction projects around the world.

Agriculture is still important in Vermont too. Dairy makes up the bulk of Vermont's farm income. The state has more than 700 dairy farms. Businesses make that milk into dairy products such as cheese or ice cream. Some Vermont dairy companies are among the most popular in the country. The Ben & Jerry's ice cream company, based in South Burlington, is famous for its creative flavors. Cabot Creamery is one of many local

JAKE BURTON CARPENTER

Jake Burton Carpenter made his first snowboard in 1977 in Londonderry, Vermont. There was a problem, though. Very few people snowboarded at the time. Those who did were often banned from local ski areas. Many viewed snowboarders as being troublemakers. Carpenter helped change that perception. His company, Burton Snowboards, became a leader in the sport. Carpenter encouraged resorts to let snowboarders in. By the 1990s the sport had exploded in popularity, even being added to the Olympics. Carpenter died in 2019, but his impact is still felt through his company. "He's like the cool dad of the sport," said Olympic gold medalist Shaun White to the *New York Times*.

cheesemakers in the state. Its Vermont Cheddar can be found in grocery stores from coast to coast.

Vermont's signature product, however, is maple syrup. No state produces more of it. The state's nearly 2 million gallons (7.6 million L) in 2018 accounted for almost half of all maple syrup produced in the United States. Most of the producers are small

Some stores in Vermont carry a wide selection of maple syrup products.

operations, with each producing less than 300 gallons (1,140 L) every year.

MANUFACTURING AND TOURISM

Today the state's biggest industry is manufacturing. Much of the state's manufacturing is done by

high-tech businesses. Companies manufacture computer and electronic products. Food and beverage products, as well as machinery, are also important.

Another big industry in Vermont is tourism. Nearly 13 million people visit Vermont each year. Many come to experience the outdoors, whether that's the summer lakes, the fall colors, or the quality ski and snowboard areas in the winter. Others might come for the state's small towns and local shops. In Vermont approximately one of every ten workers supports the tourism industry. These people often work in areas such as hotels, restaurants, and transportation.

Burlington resident Meghan Jane wrote an article giving tourists a local's perspective on the best places in town. She said:

> *You can't say you've visited Burlington unless you've been to Church St. This cobblestone street in the center of Burlington is full of life and energy. From live music to boutiques you won't find anywhere else, Church [St.] is a must when in Burlington.*
>
> *Church [St.] also features many events, including First Night (a New Year's Eve festival), an annual Christmas Tree lighting, a sidewalk sale (August), and Mardi Gras festival, to name a few.*
>
> Source: Meghan Jane. "A Local's Guide to the Best Places to Visit in Burlington, Vermont." *Wander Wisdom*, 8 Feb. 2021, wanderwisdom.com. Accessed 20 Jan. 2021.

WHAT'S THE BIG IDEA?

Jane is using evidence to support a point. What is the main point being made? Name two or three pieces of evidence Jane uses to support that point.

PEOPLE AND PLACES

People visiting Vermont often notice that it feels unique. One reason for this is that Vermont remains mostly rural. Big cities such as Boston, Massachusetts, are nearby. But Vermont is made up of mostly small cities and towns. Independent businesses and craft culture remain especially important to many Vermonters.

One quality the state lacks is diversity. More than 92 percent of people living in Vermont are non-Hispanic white. That makes

Vermont's capitol building is in Montpelier.

NATIVE CHEF

Jessee Lawyer is the head chef at a restaurant called Sweetwaters in Burlington. He's also Abenaki. One way he honors his heritage is by serving Abenaki dishes at the restaurant. The dishes use local ingredients that Abenaki people have used for generations. Many dishes include wild game. Lawyer also uses nuts and berries, as well as a variety of vegetables such as corn, squash, and sunchokes. Lawyer hopes the dishes can help people understand and appreciate American Indian cuisines. "I want to see Native families everywhere putting this on their kitchen table for them and their family," he said to Vermont Public Radio.

it one of the least diverse states in the country. Two percent are Hispanic or Latino. Asians make up 1.9 percent. Black people are only 1.4 percent of the population. Some Black and Latino people work in agriculture. The Clemmons Family Farm south of Burlington is a Black-owned farm. It celebrates Black history and culture.

STOP AND SEE IT

Burlington is Vermont's biggest city at over

44,000 people. Even when combined with neighboring cities, the area has approximately 221,000 people. This would make it a small or medium-sized city in most states. That is fitting for a state that has maintained its rural character.

As the state's cultural center, Burlington has a lot of the qualities that define the state at large. A charming downtown has many local shops and restaurants. In the summer months, people can often be found swimming or boating on Lake Champlain. The city also offers more outdoor activities, such as biking.

Few other Vermont cities have more than 20,000 people. They still have plenty to offer, though. With just over 8,000 residents, Montpelier is the nation's smallest state capital. However, it makes up for its small size with a bustling downtown area.

Rutland, in south-central Vermont, is the state's biggest city outside the Burlington area. It has more than 15,000 people. The city once known for its marble

Some people enjoy shopping and dining at businesses along Church Street in Burlington.

quarries is now a gateway to the mountains. The

Killington Ski Resort is just up the road. It's often ranked

among the best ski and snowboard areas in the country

thanks to its size and range of runs.

Downhill and cross-country skiing are popular

across the state. Stratton Mountain School in southern

Vermont had trained 46 Olympians in skiing and snowboarding by 2021. Burke Mountain Academy boasted 36 Olympians among those who trained there.

There are plenty of other outdoor activities. Vermont has 55 state parks. People from all over visit them to camp, swim, hike, fish, and boat. They can take part in snowshoeing or snowmobiling. The Lamoille Valley Rail

BERNIE SANDERS

One way Vermont has stood apart is in its progressive politics. No one has demonstrated that quite like Bernie Sanders. Though he was born in Brooklyn, New York, Sanders has lived in Vermont for most of his adult life. Identifying as a democratic socialist, Sanders did not join one of the country's two main political parties at first. Instead he was elected as an independent, first as Burlington's mayor, then as a US representative, and then as a US senator. With strong support from young voters, Sanders was the runner-up for the Democratic presidential nomination in both 2016 and 2020.

Trail runs across northern Vermont. People enjoy biking along the trail.

The state has plenty to offer those not interested in the outdoors. Historic sites dot the state. Museums have important pieces of American history. The Bennington Museum has one of the oldest Stars and Stripes flags. Or those more interested in the state's agriculture might enjoy a factory tour at Ben & Jerry's. The Green Mountain State may be small in size and population. But it has much to offer.

In 1777 Vermont became the first state to outlaw slavery. The state has never had a large Black population. Sam McReynolds, a professor of sociology, explains that one reason for this is because Vermont didn't offer qualities that would attract Black people to move there:

> *There were no jobs, there was no African-American history, heritage, culture to attract African-Americans to come to the state to settle. . . .*
>
> *What filled the mills, when they opened, the low-wage labor came from the Irish and the French Canadians. It was much easier for French Canadians to come across the border from Canada than for an African-American to make his way or her way to Vermont [from the south].*

Source: Angela Evancie and Rebecca Sananes. "Why Is Vermont So Overwhelmingly White?" *Vermont Public Radio*, 3 Mar. 2017, vpr.org. Accessed 1 Feb. 2021.

BACK IT UP

McReynolds is using evidence to support a point. Write a paragraph describing the point he is making. Then write down two or three pieces of evidence he uses to make the point.

IMPORTANT DATES

11,000–9,000 years ago
Paleo-Indians move into the area that's now Vermont following the last Ice Age.

1609
French explorer Samuel de Champlain is the first European to visit the lake now called Lake Champlain.

1666
The first French settlement in Vermont, Fort Sainte Anne, is established on Isle La Motte on Lake Champlain.

1724
The first permanent European settlement in Vermont is developed near today's Brattleboro.

1775
The Green Mountain Boys help capture Fort Ticonderoga in one of the first major colonial wins during the Revolutionary War.

1791

Vermont becomes the fourteenth state.

2018

Almost half of all maple syrup produced in the United States comes from Vermont.

2020

Vermont independent senator Bernie Sanders is the runner-up for the Democratic presidential nomination for the second time.

Tell the Tale

Chapter Three discusses the plants and animals in Vermont. Write 200 words about visiting a Vermont forest. What plants and animals do you see? What is the weather like?

Dig Deeper

Some wonder how one of the most progressive states and the first to abolish slavery could be the least diverse. With an adult's help, find a few reliable sources that help explain why Vermont remained prominently white after the Civil War. Then find sources about what the state is doing to become more diverse and why it's important to the people of Vermont.

Take a Stand

From enjoying winter sports to shopping from local farmers and craftspeople, there is a lot to do in Vermont. Which activity described in this book do you think is the most fun, and why?

Why Do I Care?

Perhaps you are not interested in learning about a state's industries. But that doesn't mean you can't think about how certain industries affect your life. How would your life be different if one of the industries mentioned in Chapter Four did not exist?

GLOSSARY

democratic socialist
someone who believes companies should be owned by the employees

economy
a place's system of goods, services, money, and jobs

erode
to wear away by the movement of wind, water, or other natural forces

hydroelectric
electricity generated from flowing water

militia
a group of citizens who form a military force

progressive
a political belief that strong government action can lead to positive social changes

quarry
an open area where stones or minerals are dug up

rural
having to do with the countryside

title
an official document showing something's owner

ONLINE RESOURCES

To learn more about Vermont, visit our free resource websites below.

Visit **abdocorelibrary.com** or scan this QR code for free Common Core resources for teachers and students, including vetted activities, multimedia, and booklinks, for deeper subject comprehension.

Visit **abdobooklinks.com** or scan this QR code for free additional online weblinks for further learning. These links are routinely monitored and updated to provide the most current information available.

LEARN MORE

Bell, Samantha S. *Exploring New England*. Abdo, 2018.

Krull, Kathleen. *A Kid's Guide to the American Revolution*. HarperCollins, 2018.

INDEX

About the Author

Casey Englund is a children's book author and avid bicyclist who lives in Minnesota with a cuddly Lab named Marquette.